THE MUTE SWAN

JANET KEAR

CONTENTS
Introduction 2
The Swan's year 4
The Polish swan 11
Food and feeding 15
Death 19
Swans and man 21
Places to visit 24
Further reading 24

COVER: *A female Mute Swan at her nest with a newly hatched cygnet beside her. Her relatively small bill knob distinguishes her from the male. The rusty colour of her head and neck indicates that she has been feeding in water containing iron salts.*

Series editors: Jim Flegg and Chris Humphries.

Copyright © 1988 by Janet Kear. First published 1988.
Number 27 in the Shire Natural History series. ISBN 0 85263 948 1.

All rights reserved. No part of this publication may be reproduced or transmitted in any form or by any means, electronic or mechanical, including photocopy, recording, or any information storage and retrieval system, without permission in writing from the publishers, Shire Publications Ltd, Cromwell House, Church Steet, Princes Risborough, Aylesbury, Bucks HP17 9AJ, UK.

Set in 9 point Times roman and printed in Great Britain by C. I. Thomas & Sons (Haverfordwest) Ltd, Press Buildings, Merlins Bridge, Haverfordwest, Dyfed.

Introduction

The Mute Swan is Britain's largest bird and one of the world's heavier flying animals. It is as familiar to most people as the Robin. It is graceful, confiding and much loved.

The Mute Swan *(Cygnus olor)* is distributed throughout Europe and Asia and has been introduced into South Africa, North America and Australia by homesick immigrants. In the continental parts of its range it is often migratory, with wintering and breeding grounds that do not overlap. The British population, however, is usually sedentary although at times of severe weather it may be joined by swans from the east. Most of this book concerns the Mute Swan in Britain, where the bird is widespread and associated with almost any area of fresh water. The only restrictions to its watery habitat are that the pond or stream cannot be so small (less than about 20 metres or yards) that the birds are unable to take off, and nests are not normally found in hilly country above 300 metres (1000 feet). Probably there have always been wild Mute Swans in Britain but some authorities suggest that the present population derives from birds brought back from the Crusades and partly domesticated at the time of Richard the Lionheart (reigned 1189-99).

In Scandinavia and north Germany populations are mainly migratory and the largest concentrations of swans occur between the coasts of Denmark and Sweden during the moult in July, August and September. Birds may winter in southern Sweden and southern Germany or, as the weather becomes colder, move west into Denmark, Schleswig-Holstein and occasionally into the Netherlands, Belgium and northern France. The small, rather isolated, populations of central Europe also move in winter; for instance, birds breeding in the southern USSR winter on the coasts of the Black and Caspian seas.

What are the Mute Swan's nearest relatives? Surprisingly, its closest cousin is probably the Black Swan *(Cygnus atratus)* of Australia and New Zealand, with which it has bred and produced hybrid young. As well as being the only swan lacking much white plumage, the Black Swan is unusual in that it nests in colonies and the male bird does a substantial amount of the incubation of the eggs. The Mute Swan and the Black Swan, however, share a threat display which consists of raising the secondary feathers of the wings, presumably in order to make the bird look as large and menacing as possible. All other aggressive swans keep their wings tight against their bodies as they charge forward towards the object of their wrath. Among the other swan species, the Mute is probably closer in relationship to the Black-necked Swan *(C. melanocoryphus)* of South America than it is to the 'northern white swans': the Trumpeter Swan *(C. cygnus buccinator)*, Whooper Swan *(C. cygnus cygnus)*, Whistling Swan *(C. columbianus columbianus)* and Bewick's Swan *(C. columbianus bewickii)*. Unlike these four, the male and female Mute Swans can be distinguished because of a greater disparity in size between the sexes, and also by a larger knob on the bill of the male (or cob) than that of the female (or pen). There is also a difference in voice: although the Mute can utter a series of snores, snorts and hisses, it lacks the bugle-like, carrying calls of the northern swans. However, the bird makes a loud pulsing noise with its wings, and families probably keep together by listening for the sound of their neighbour's pinions as they fly, instead of by calling as do the other swans.

At close range the Mute Swan is unlikely to be confused with the two other British swans, the Whooper and Bewick's. Its bill is orange and black rather than yellow and black, its neck is more gracefully curved, its wings are shorter so that its tail appears to be carried more erect, and it frequently arches the secondary feathers over its back. If a swan is seen in summer, it is almost certainly a Mute; the Whooper and Bewick's are migratory, occurring in Scotland and England only between late September and April, and nesting at more northerly latitudes. In winter the Mute Swan is less likely to be seen feeding on land than the other two

1. *Cob, or male, Mute Swan showing the bill knob that is largest in the mature, breeding bird. The skin area between the eye and the bill is naked of feathers in all adult swans. This bird has been preening and has a down plumule adhering to its bill.*

species, as it is clumsy and moves with more difficulty once out of the water.

All swans belong to the wildfowl family (Anatidae, or duck-like birds) and among these their nearest relatives are the grazing geese, with whom they share a number of behaviour patterns, particularly a well developed family life and a firm bond between the adult pair. Swans and geese are classified in the tribe *Anserini*. They are probably more primitive than the ducks and certainly are among the largest of the wildfowl. The anserine tribe includes some 23 species in four genera: *Anser* or grey geese, *Branta* or black geese, *Cygnus*, the swans, and *Coscoroba*, an unusual swan-like bird from South America. In the course of evolution swans probably appeared first, and a line from them eventually gave rise to the geese. The true geese are confined to the northern hemisphere; swans are found in both hemispheres and are rare only in the tropics.

Differences between swans and geese are mostly matters of degree — a relatively larger foot or longer neck — but the groups also differ slightly in behaviour. Swans are all larger than geese, and the adults have naked lores, which are the areas between the bill and the eyes. They incubate their eggs for longer (the Black Swan for 39 days), take longer to fledge and never breed until they are at least three years old, while a female goose can lay when she is only two. The male swan helps build the nest, a type of parental care that is absent in the male goose (or gander). Swans also provide some food for their newly hatched young by plucking underwater or overhead vegetation, and by foot paddling to bring edible items to the surface, while three swan species, including the Mute Swan, carry their cygnets on their backs in the early stages.

The swan's year

A pair of Mute Swans will probably be on territory by February and that territory will usually be a stretch of river or lake shore, a few metres wide and perhaps 250-300 metres (270-330 yards) long. The male in particular will be defending its boundaries from other swans (and from everything that might be mistaken for a swan, such as a white goose or white duck) by a display called 'busking' and, if necessary, by fighting. Two busking males will parade the shared edge of their domains by swimming up and down, the secondary feathers of the wings raised, neck feathers on end and heads laid back, making themselves as conspicuous as possible. The bird's white plumage is in itself a form of advertisement announcing to others the presence of a territory owner and keeping them at a distance. If after a show of strength one rival does not turn and swim away with sleeked neck, wings flat on the back and bill pointing down, then fighting may result. The birds bite one another around the neck and shoulders and strike with the 'wrists' of the raised wings. Although most fights end without bloodshed, because one male gives in, about 3 per cent of annual adult mortality is thought to be due to attacks at territory boundaries. A large cob is capable of killing another swan or even a small dog. His reaction to man depends mainly on how familiar he is with him; individual swans that have been reared close to humans, and perhaps had experience of a particularly aggressive father, can be very fierce in defence of their nests. They are best given a wide berth in the breeding season.

Some male Mutes (probably not all, as the behaviour has been noticed and described only recently) indicate that they are in possession of a territory by a loud foot-slapping display. The cob may do it every time he alights in his territory, or when he is already on the pond, and especially if an intruding male swan lands. The bird runs across the water, slapping the surface and flapping his wings. This makes a noise that carries some distance and also has a conspicuous visual impact. Other young birds may associate the display with being chased by a dominant male and keep away.

In a few places the Mute Swan nests colonially but this is uncommon. Abbotsbury in Dorset, on the tidal Fleet, has the only important colony in Britain. It is thought to have been established centuries ago to stock the larders of the monks, and it survives only because of some feeding by man and an abundant supply of natural food for the cygnets and their parents. This food is mainly *Zostera marina*, or Eel Grass, an herbaceous flowering plant that looks rather like seaweed and grows in mud or sand from spring-tide low water down to a depth of 4 metres (13 feet). Abbotsbury birds are less aggressive than those elsewhere and this character seems to be inherited.

The swan pair will have been formed in a winter flock when the male was nearly three years old and the female typically a year younger. Courtship tends not to be very obvious (mostly consisting of mutual head turning, breast to breast) and is especially inconspicuous in older birds that have been together for many years. The pair, once formed, stays together through the breeding and winter seasons. A stable bond is essential, as the family of cygnets will need solicitude and guidance for about seven months, so some display between cob and pen can be seen as the nesting season approaches. Divorce is rare (less than 10 per cent), and particularly so once the pair has been successful in rearing young. Copulation seems to be important in maintaining the relationship, most pairs mating far more often than is necessary to fertilise the clutch. Both birds alternately dip their heads beneath the water and preen or rub the back and flanks. Gradually the two synchronise their activities and, between dippings, hold their necks upright and close together for a moment or two. The wings are low, often dragging in the water, and the cob pushes his neck and body over the female's until he is on her back hanging on to her neck feathers with his bill. After mating he slips off and both birds give a low snort. They half rise from the water, necks extended and bills point-

2. *An adult Whooper Swan, a migratory relative of the Mute Swan that is present in Britain only in the winter and is more often seen on land. The Mute Swan spends relatively more of its time on the water.*

3. *A pair of male Mute Swans swimming side by side in threat display at the edge of their territories. The nearer bird is slightly more aggressive (wings held higher and neck feathers on end) so the parade may be taking place closer to his nest site.*

4. *A clutch of six eggs laid in a nest of reeds and other plant stems that is constructed by both parents.*

ing first up, then down and finally from side to side. Both partners then bathe, tail-wag and preen.

By mid March the pair will be building a nest. If on dry land, the nest is almost always within 90 metres (100 yards) of the water's edge, generally less, and occasionally it is surrounded by water in, for instance, a reed bed. Nest sites are frequently re-used if eggs were hatched there the previous year, and the pile of sticks, rushes and grass takes about ten days to construct. Considerable quantities of material may be moved by both birds; the male brings vegetation from a distance while his mate stands on the nest site arranging what he passes to her. Material is not carried to the nest; it is picked up and passed backwards over the shoulder or beside the feet.

Eggs are laid at the rate of one every 48 hours, usually in the morning. They are large, weighing about 345 grams (12 ounces) each, which makes them the equivalent of seven domestic hen's eggs and the largest of any British bird. A clutch of six is normal, but eleven have been recorded in one nest. Younger swans will lay fewer eggs than older birds, so an especially big clutch will belong to a well established and well fed pair.

For 36 days from the laying of the last egg the female sits on her clutch while the cob is at hand to repel unwelcome visitors. She leaves to feed about once every 24 hours but otherwise passes the time asleep, with bill tip tucked in the feathers of her back, or gathers and arranges material within reach of her nest. Among white swans, only the female incubates, although occasionally the cob sits on the nest while she is absent. Whether the cob broods (that is, applies heat to the eggs) on these occasions is uncertain. He may just sit on the clutch while guarding it. Hatching starts with the last egg to be laid, and all the youngsters have left their shells within 36 hours. They have pale grey down and are somewhat unsteady on their feet. They are relatively large, weighing about 220 grams (7¾ ounces) and more than 25 per cent of their body weight consists of a yolk sac. This yolk is drawn into the abdomen of the cygnet during the hatching process. It is rich in fats and protein that will provide nourishment during the first week of life.

Like all young waterfowl, cygnets accept as parents the first large moving objects that they see and follow them in preference to anything else. This process of learning is called *imprinting*. On the second morning after hatching mother and father lead their cygnets to water. The family may return to the nest at night but usually from now on the parents will brood their young by carrying them on their backs between the folded wings. Here they can sleep warmly and safely, away from the cold and from underwater predators suck as pike and large eels. The cygnets climb on at a point between the tips of the short folded wings and the tail. They are not helped aboard except that the adult stays still and may form a step with the 'heel' of the foot. Both parents participate, although the male does less carrying than his mate, and the carrying depends largely on the young themselves. A Mute Swan cygnet that the author hand-reared was restless sitting in her lap; it showed a strong inclination to climb and always reached her shoulder before settling down.

The cygnet's husky voice is important in telling its parents that it is lost, cold, sleepy, hurt, threatened or content, and in eliciting the appropriate response. Communication with the mother, and with brothers and sisters in the brood, starts while the young are still in the egg about two days before hatching. First clicks are heard, then cheeps; the female responds by calling softly and presumably both parent and cygnets become familiar with one another's voices.

Although the size of males and females at hatching is similar (both weighing on average 220 grams or 7¾ ounces), weights start to diverge at about two weeks and males will grow faster than their sisters. The first feathers appear at about five weeks of age on the shoulders and under the wings. Next come those on the belly, the flanks and, finally, those on the head and neck. At the time of fledging, perhaps by the middle of October, males are on average 28 per cent heavier than females. This is considerably more than the difference between the sexes in male and female Bewick's or Whooper Swans.

The cygnets will not fly until they are about twenty weeks old, by which time they will have lost all their down and acquired a brown first plumage. Through

5. *A pair of Mute Swans with their cygnets at the nest. Both parents are threatening the photographer with raised wings and feathers of the neck on end. The cob, which has the larger bill knob, is in the foreground.*

6. *A male Mute Swan in threat display towards the photographer. His relatively large bill knob distinguishes him from the female. Like most ducks, geese and swans, he uses only one eye for close observation.*

the autumn and early winter these drab brown feathers are gradually moulted and replaced by white ones. Additional white birds in their territory are not welcomed by the adult swans, and it seems that the cygnets are persuaded to fly off to join a juvenile flock elsewhere. Sometimes, however, as cold weather arrives, the whole family migrates a short distance to a common wintering area where there is ample food. Outside the breeding season, birds of all ages may be gregarious. In Britain, winter groups tend to be rather small. Over 90 per cent of the sites surveyed in the winter wildfowl counts organised by the Wildfowl Trust held fewer than 25 Mute Swans, and 98.6 per cent had fewer than 100. On the other hand, in continental countries, notably Denmark, coastal wintering flocks may consist of thousands of individuals. British wintering sites may be public parks, where bread offered by humans is an important dietary item, rivers and brackish estuaries. Some Mutes also gather to feed at brewery outfalls or distilleries that discharge waste grain into waterways.

Parent birds leave these winter flocks in February to return to the territory and start the process of reproduction again. Their cygnets remain behind, and brothers and sisters may associate with other families of juveniles during the following summer and winter. Although the youngster's feathers are usually entirely white by its second winter, its bill remains leaden blue in colour for another six months before gradually becoming the orange and black of the adult bird.

Swans, like ducks and geese, are flightless for a month or so every summer because all the primary and secondary wing feathers, or quills, are moulted at the same time. This flightless period occurs after nesting, while the cygnets are still fairly young. The male moults first, and then the female, so that although the family stays on the comparative safety of

7. Juvenile Mute Swans in their first winter plumage.

8. A pair of Mute Swans upending to feed on underwater vegetation.

9. *A female Mute Swan carrying and brooding her small cygnets on her back beneath her wings. The bird's tail feathers are unusually frayed and worn but will be replaced at the next moult in June.*

the water there is usually one parent able-bodied for defence. Non-breeding birds move to a new wetland site for the moult and gather on the water in quite large numbers, especially on the continent. These moult migrations are to places that are particularly safe for the flightless birds and have a good supply of

10. *A brood of cygnets, about ten days old, feeding in shallow water. The area between the eye and the bill is covered with down at this stage.*

11. *A flock of adult Mute Swans taking off from a Danish lake. The birds run along the surface of the water for a short distance and after take-off extend legs and feet along the body beside the tail.*

underwater vegetation for food. In Britain the largest moulting concentration, around five to seven hundred birds, is on the Fleet near Abbotsbury, where the main food is *Zostera* and the green alga *Enteromorpha*.

The primary feathers are dropped some days before the secondaries and then grow in at slightly different rates, the primaries faster (at about 6 mm or ¼ inch per day) than the secondaries, so that their replacement is more or less synchronised. The swans can fly once more three or four weeks before their flight feathers have attained full length; their body weight is at its lowest and this also helps to reduce the period of flightlessness during which they are relatively defenceless.

Young Mute Swans may find a mate when they are two years old, but the cob will not usually breed until he is four and the female not until she is three. So there is often a difference of one year in the ages of the mated pair.

The Polish swan

Cygnets in first plumage are brown, but there is an important exception to this rule among individuals known as 'Polish swans'. The first time this phenomenon was recorded in print, at the end of the seventeenth century, the birds were on the river Trent at Rugeley, Staffordshire. They were described as having pink legs and feet instead of black ones. Later it was found that there was a difference in the colour of the cygnets' down as well. The young hatched white instead of grey and the juvenile birds had feathers that were as white as those of the adult. W. Yarrell, in a paper published in 1841, pronounced them to be a new, slightly smaller species which he called *Cygnus immutabilis*, or the Changeless Swan, because the first and subsequent plumages were the same. The name 'Polish

12 (above). *A family of Mute Swans about ten days after hatching. The male parent is in the foreground.*

13 (below). *An adult Mute Swan preening beneath its wing.*
14 (right). *The same bird shakes its wings after preening.*

15. *Normal winter range and regular wintering areas from an International Waterfowl Research Bureau census carried out from 1967 to 1976.*

swan' was given to the birds by London poulterers who imported them from the Baltic; the condition is not commonly seen in Britain but is much more usual in continental Europe, as the designation 'Polish' implies. In Holland it was first recorded near Haarlem in 1840 and is now common throughout the country. On Lake Geneva the first white cygnets were noted in 1868; by 1899, no less than 28 per cent of the population had the characteristic pale feet. The introduced Mute Swans in Rhode Island, USA, likewise tend to have a large proportion of white offspring. Here a few pairs were introduced in the 1940s and by 1967 there were approximately six hundred, of which 17 per cent were Polish.

The affected birds have a deficiency of the black pigment, melanin, caused by a recessive sex-linked gene. The inheritance of any attribute is controlled by genes carried on paired chromosomes, and the two chromosomes that make up any pair are normally identical. The determination of any animal's sex is by means of one pair of chromosomes; in female birds (but in male mammals) the pair of sex chromosomes is not identical — the odd member of this pair is called W (or Y) and the other Z (or X), so that the female has a WZ combination and the male ZZ. The W chromosome carries few genes and is often effectively inert. The Z chromosome, on the other hand, carries the normal complement of genes affecting characters other than gender, and these characters are therefore linked to the sex of the individual. In birds sex-linked traits appear much more commonly in females than in males. In mammals it is the other way round, and sex-linked characters, like haemophilia and colour-blindness, are more common in men than in women. In Mute Swans the condition of melanin deficiency that results in white down and pink feet is three times more frequent in pens than in cobs. Therefore the reason why Yarrell considered that Polish swans were smaller on average then ordinary Mute Swans was that most of those he saw were smaller because they were females.

There are several records of parents attacking their white cygnets if most of their other offspring were brown. It might seem surprising, therefore, that the condition survives if a cygnet lacking a brown juvenile plumage has no protection from its father's assaults. Surely, a white youngster is less likely to grow up and pass on its genes to the next generation? Can there be some compensating gain, especially for females? It has been suggested that there is and that this is related to the fact that the pen is often a year younger than her mate, the cob, when the pair bond is formed. The young white Polish female appears older than she is. She can thus attract a male earlier than normal, perhaps as early as her first winter. She can spend her second (infertile) spring gaining experience of a partner and of a territory and nest successfully during the following year. Thus, in comparison with her normally coloured sisters, the Polish swan can extend her breeding lifespan by a year, and her sex-linked gene will confer a net profit in terms of offspring produced, despite parental aggression.

The domestication of the Mute Swan also may have encouraged the spread of the gene for whiteness. In Holland, swans were bred selectively by man and the juveniles sold either alive as ornamental birds or dead for meat and skins; the normal brown cygnet was not nearly so valuable, especially for the trade in swans-down. In other countries the carcases were sold without being skinned and it was the tender brown birds that were selected for the pot. The white juveniles may have been presumed to be adult and allowed to grow on and reproduce.

Melanin deficiency occurs occasionally in some other swans and results in the same pinkish legs and feet and a pale first plumage. Although no pink-legged Whooper Swans have been seen recently in Britain, Bewick's Swans with white cygnets and flesh-coloured legs are reported occasionally, and Trumpeter Swans in Yellowstone National Park, Wyoming, USA, are similarly affected. We are familiar with the condition in a few garden birds, such as Blackbirds, and in domestic poultry, but only in the Mute Swan is the character quite common and known to be controlled by a sex-linked gene. A deficiency of melanin, but not of any other of the bird's normal pigments, is usually referred to as 'leucism', and the individual is called 'leucistic'. A complete lack of colour is 'albinism' and is much rarer. An albino bird has pink eyes, as well as a pink bill and feet and often seems to suffer from impaired vision. An affected bird would therefore not be expected to survive long in the wild.

Food and feeding

The Mute Swan has a typical waterfowl bill but it is larger than most. It is provided with fine lamellae, or comb-like structures, that lie in parallel rows along the upper and lower edges and along the sides of the fleshy tongue. There is a rounded tip with a pair of hard 'nails' used for gouging pieces out of hard food such as tubers. Although basically a

16. *The webbed foot of the Mute Swan.*
17. *The webbed foot of the Polish Mute Swan.*

SHIRE PUBLICATIONS specialises in publishing inexpensive book about unusual aspects of our heritage, rural life, industrial and social history, old transport, folklore and crafts, architecture and garden history, archaeology, topography, fashion and needlecrafts, antiques and collecting, ethnography and natural history.

If you would like to receive details of other Shire Publications, please complete and post this card.

Name ....

Address ....

....

....

Post code ....

Special interests *(please tick relevant boxes)*
- ☐ Antiques and collecting
- ☐ Archaeology
- ☐ Architecture
- ☐ Canals and Ships
- ☐ Egyptology
- ☐ Ethnography
- ☐ Fashion and needlecraft
- ☐ Garden history
- ☐ Industrial archaeology
- ☐ Military history
- ☐ Natural history
- ☐ Road transport

Any other (please state) ....
....

POST CARD

SHIRE PUBLICATIONS LTD.

CROMWELL HOUSE

CHURCH STREET

PRINCES RISBOROUGH

AYLESBURY

BUCKINGHAMSHIRE

HP17 9AJ

U.K.

18. *Two cygnets floating with their feet lifted up beneath their growing wings. The leading bird has the normal grey-brown colour; the one behind is Polish and lacks any melanin pigment.*

19. *A family in which one cygnet is Polish, lacking the normal grey-brown down. Sometimes the adults will attack the white cygnet.*

vegetarian browser, the swan is happiest feeding while afloat. It frequently upends to reach plants and their roots beneath about 1 metre (3 feet) of water and has a long flexible neck containing 25 vertebrae — more than any other bird or mammal. It also grazes on land, takes grain from stubble fields and filters small seed and duckweed from the water surface. The Mute Swan also adapts well to being fed by humans, and the artificial provision of winter food has been an important factor in the growth of swan populations. In order to grind down its food in its gizzard before digestion (no bird has teeth), the Mute Swan takes grit in the form of small stones and sand. Because of the presence of salt-extracting glands beneath the skin above the eyes, it is able to drink sea water and feed on the coast, particularly in hard weather. Many other waterbirds have these same salt glands and they are particularly well developed in sea ducks such as eiders and scoters. All British swans may be found on the coast in the winter and the glands are often noticeably swollen in birds that have been feeding on inter-tidal vegetation. Salt is removed from the bloodstream and excreted in concentrated solution through the nostrils; drops then run to the tip of the bill and are flicked off by the bird shaking its head.

In winter less than 50 per cent on average of the food of the Mute Swan consists of underwater vegetation, whereas in summer over 80 per cent is soft plants that are dredged from beneath the surface. *Zostera*, the marine Eel Grass, is a favourite food where it is abundant. Stomachs of Mute Swans from the Ouse Washes in East Anglia that have been killed in accidents have been found to contain various soft grasses such as Marsh Foxtail *(Alopecurus geniculatus)*, Creeping Bent *(Agrostis stolonifera)* and Floating Sweet Grass *(Glyceria fluitans)*. Aquatic flowering plants such as Starwort *(Callitriche)*, Hornwort *(Ceratophyllum demersum)* and Water Crowfoot *(Ranunculus)* are eaten, as well as the starchy roots of Marsh Yellow-Cress *(Rorippa palustre)*. More analyses have been made of stomach contents in Sweden and Denmark in winter. Here, too, submerged vegetation is the main constituent of the diet, including Stonewort *(Chara)*, Wigeon Grass *(Ruppia potamogeton)* and Water Milfoil *(Myriophyllum)*. It has been calculated that just over 2 kg (4½

20. *A pair of Mute Swans, the male in front, feeding while wading in shallow water.*

pounds) of fresh grass will be needed by the average Mute Swan per day. This is not taken evenly throughout the 24 hours, and undisturbed swans have been found to increase their feeding activity during the day and to continue to feed after dark. Presumably they find their food by touch and taste rather than by sight.

Their wasteful method of feeding often results in long drift lines of severed vegetation gathering behind a party of upending swans. These are utilised by a variety of waterbirds which lack a long reach and so cannot so easily exploit the deeper levels, among them Wigeon, Coot and Little Grebes.

The cygnets in their first three weeks of life take rather more high-protein animal matter, especially water insects, than they will later. They are helped to find their food by the parents pulling vegetation from beneath the water, from the bank or from overhanging branches and dropping it on the surface. In doing so, the adults dislodge water boatmen, beetles and other small animals, and these are gobbled up by the cygnets.

Another behaviour pattern that increases in a breeding pair of Mute Swans is foot paddling or trampling. Many waterbirds do this occasionally, usually when standing in shallow water, in order to raise particles of food to the surface. Parent swans paddle a lot, and edible items are taken eagerly by the cygnets. The adults seem to make the association between trampling and food for the young: if a family of Mute Swans is ashore at a place where they are often fed by humans, then one or both of the parents may be seen to be marking time with their feet even before the food arrives. They appear to be performing in an almost nervous way, and it has been suggested that the paddling movement has the additional function of attracting the young to their parent's side and so keeps the family together.

Gradually the cygnets will eat fewer invertebrates and more and more vegetation and, by two weeks of age, they start pulling and severing their own food. By the seventh day a young Mute Swan is able to dip its head under water and hold it there for just under two seconds. This increases to an average of six seconds at twenty-eight days and seven and a half seconds at sixty days. Upending begins at about ten days but is brief and clumsy, and even during its first autumn the juvenile bird is upending for shorter periods than its parents.

Death

Many cygnets die in the second week of life, when the yolk that they hatched with is used up. During those two weeks they must learn to feed efficiently and a few never do so. After leaving their parents seven or eight months later, juveniles are again at great risk; in their first winter and second summer young birds are three times more likely to die than adults. This higher mortality may be related to the fact that youngsters fly around more than older swans, although in Britain, few Mutes move more than 50 km (30 miles) from the place where they were hatched.

Human beings affect the Mute Swan very greatly. Collision with man-made objects used to be the commonest cause of death in all British swans; power lines are an especial hazard. From reports collected in the middle 1960s, of 1050 dead Mute Swans, for instance, it was found that 65 per cent had collided with man-made objects, and two-thirds of these collisions were with overhead wires. A bird as heavy as a Mute Swan, which can weigh 16 kg (35 pounds), although the average is 11.9 kg (26 pounds), cannot readily see a narrow wire in time to take avoiding action. Marking wires, often with corks or plastic spirals, makes them more visible and benefits man by reducing the number of electricity power failures.

Another man-made object has become a greater danger for the Mute Swan in southern Britain. Lead poisoning has resulted in an estimated four thousand deaths a year and a 40 per cent reduction of birds on many large English and Welsh rivers like the Thames, the Dee, the Warwickshire Avon and the Bristol Avon. The poisoning results from the bird eating anglers' discarded split lead

21. *Swan upping on the river Thames at Marlow, Buckinghamshire.*

shot in mistake for grit. The grinding action of the gizzard and the digestive acids break down and dissolve the metal so that it is absorbed into the bloodstream. The effect of lead poisoning is paralysis, and the bird dies a slow death as its muscles fail — it cannot walk properly, fly, hold up its head or pass its food down its gut. The British government imposed a ban on the sale of lead sinkers used in freshwater fishing from January 1987. Non-toxic substitute weights have been available as an alternative to lead since 1984 and, if all anglers use them, many unnecessary swan deaths will be avoided in areas where coarse fishing is common.

Oil pollution is also a hazard, especially in winter when large numbers of birds gather downstream in estuaries, for instance. Boating, dredging and similar interference with their wetland habitat have been blamed for locally declining swan populations. Man frequently makes life difficult for all waterbirds. Nevertheless, the population of Mute Swans in Britain as a whole was about 18,900 in 1983 and, because the birds are doing well in some parts of Scotland where life is not so risky, total numbers were found to be rising slightly. Swans, because of their large size and white plumage, are among the easiest birds to count accurately and a number of censuses of the United Kingdom population have been made since 1955, when the first was organised by the British Trust for Ornithology. There were then between 14,300 and 15,300 birds, with 3500 to 4000 in Scotland, including 463 known nesting pairs. Those on the Outer Hebrides, although originally introduced, are now essentially wild. Breeding success there is good, especially of pairs on lakes with plenty of vegetation, and density is higher than it is elsewhere in Britain. Swans are comparatively long-lived; occasional birds may live as long as 21 years, although 96 per cent are dead by the age of ten. The suggestion is that a pair of Mute Swans takes an average of five breeding seasons to produce the two adult replacements that are needed to maintain a stable population. The total population of Britain, northern and central Europe is estimated to be 140,000.

Swans and man

Much of the information gathered about swans, their reproduction and mortality, and about the distance they travel in a lifetime, is obtainable only if the individual bird carries a ring on its leg. The standard ring, issued by the British Trust for Ornithology, is made of a light alloy and stamped with a serial number and the address of the British Museum, to which the finder of the swan may write. Most such recoveries depend on the finding of a dead body, because the number on the ring cannot be read at a range of more than a few metres. Since the mid 1960s the Wildfowl Trust has developed the use of large plastic leg rings for swans, with numbers or letters that can be read with binoculars at a distance of 90 metres (100 yards) or so. A study of the colonial nesting Mute Swans at Abbotsbury, which started in 1968, has depended on these visible coloured bands that eliminate the need for repeated catches of the same bird.

Some interesting differences have been found between the Abbotsbury swans and the more usual territorial ones breeding elsewhere in Britain. The nesting season starts later and the clutch contains on average fewer eggs. Many of the cygnets are reared artificially; the first broods to hatch are put with their parents into swan pens and further young are added until the pens may contain as many as 140 cygnets, with only seven pairs of adults accompanying them. Food is given until mid September, when the birds are released (in the old days they would have been fattened for Christmas and New Year). Survival of these well fed juveniles during the subsequent winter and summer can be very high — as high as that of adults — and much better than that of other young swans in the British population.

Mute Swans can be easily caught during late July and early August, when the cygnets are too young to fly and the adults are moulting their wings. They can then be herded into temporary pens and removed individually to be marked. They require careful and firm handling, as they can hurt both themselves and the researcher. Often, however, they are tame enough to be caught by hand (if that hand is also offering bread) or by a crook on a long pole.

Feeding by man has resulted in a great expansion in the numbers of Mute Swans overwintering in Britain and was probably responsible for the population increase that occurred in the 1950s. Winter is frequently a time of great trial for waterbirds and starvation is possible if the water freezes. The feeding of wild birds became common as public interest was aroused in natural history subjects by television; this reduced the possibility of starvation, especially among immature birds, and populations increased (only to be cut back again, in the case of swans, by power lines and lead). Meanwhile winter feeding became widespread in Poland, Germany and other European countries, and Mute Swan numbers rose there too. Food offered in winter is most effective in keeping inland swans in good condition. Much of it is bread and grain given directly by the local human population to 'their' swans, but some increase in winter provisioning has been accidental — from outfalls of brewery waste and at the source of heated open water at power stations and industrial effluent discharges for instance. Feeding by man naturally favours the least shy birds. In Britain swans have been adapted for many centuries to a semi-domestic way of life. This was less the case on the European continent, where some selection of birds that could thrive in the proximity of humans seems to have occurred along with great increases in total numbers since the 1950s, and especially during the 1970s. In a study in Sweden it was found that the heaviest birds in winter were the ones most likely to breed the following spring, and that there was a clear relationship between the weight of the female and the number of eggs laid in the clutch. The larger birds must often be the oldest ones, since it has already been noted that large clutches are usually the property of well established pairs.

Mute Swans were farmed in Britain from the twelfth century. Cygnets were taken from their parents at about three months of age and put in special pits to be fattened for Christmas or for feasts such as weddings. They became closely associated with the monarchy and acquired a snob value for others. Edward IV decreed that, except for sons of the king, only freeholders of land above a certain value could own and mark swans; all others belonged to the Crown.

Before the turkey was imported from America in the sixteenth century ordinary people ate goose as a special meal. The upper classes were served with roast swan; they gave swans as gifts of distinction and graced their estates with a 'game' of swans. The adult birds were all pinioned and so could not fly, and they presumably did not swim great distances, but no one seems to have tried to control which swans mated and nested. Thus true domestication, with deliberate selection by man of features that suited him, did not occur. A Swan Master and numerous deputies throughout Britain were appointed by the king to oversee the division of the cygnets that resulted from the breeding season before any young could fly away. The birds were divided according to clearly laid-down rules. The possible owners had to be present, so the Swan Master or his deputy had to be responsible for informing all interested parties, organising the boats and managing the swan-catching programme.

If the parents of the cygnets both belonged to the same landowner and they had nested on his property, then he could claim them all. If they had nested on someone else's land, then a single cygnet (called the 'ground bird') went to that person as land rent. If, however, he was a freeholder of insufficient property to own swans at all, then he was paid the value of the cygnet by someone who had the privilege of keeping them and who added that bird to his own collection. When the pen and cob belonged to different owners, the brood (after payment of the ground bird, if necessary) was split between them, and the owner of the male had the first choice. If the remaining cygnets were an odd number, then disposal of the extra bird seems to have been subject to local custom. In Fenland it went to the owner of the cob, as being 'the more worthy'. On the Thames it was valued and whoever took it paid the owner of the other parent half the agreed amount. Sometimes two owners took it in turns annually to claim the odd cygnet.

Swan-keeping declined through the eighteenth century as it was expensive and preferred foods became widely available. The Mute Swan had two drawbacks as a farmed animal. Firstly, it was aggressive and could not be maintained normally at a high density and, secondly, it had to have access to water. The performance of rounding them up was difficult and time-consuming compared to dealing with a flock of geese or turkeys. Their value was correspondingly high: in 1315 a breeding pair and five other swans were said to be worth £10 — a goose would cost perhaps 3d.

Swan-upping, when all swans are counted and the cygnets are pinioned and their bills marked, now takes place only on the river Thames in July, while the adults are in wing moult and the youngsters have not yet fledged. Bill marks, like large plastic rings, are conspicuous enough to be seen from a distance so that ownership can be confirmed without any need to catch the bird repeatedly. The marks are scars that result from cuts made with a sharp knife in the soft tissue of (usually) the bird's upper mandible. In the sixteenth and seventeenth centuries, between one and eight notches might have been cut in one or both margins. More elaborate variations included initials and heraldic devices, and these were made across the centre of the bill. As many as 630 marks were in use between 1450 and 1600. The only 'royalties' in swans now remaining, which confer a right to own and mark on the Thames, are those granted to the Dyers and the Vintners livery companies. The bills of the cygnets are marked with one notch for the Dyers, two notches for the Vintners, while any royal birds are left unmarked.

For many centuries there were almost no wild Mute Swans in Britain: they were all owned by someone and were pinioned. The sound and sight of a flying bird, producing a loud pulsating sound with its wing feathers, is a relatively modern experience. Pinioning is the amputation of the last section of one wing, so that the primaries never develop on that side and the bird is unbalanced as it tries to take off. The practice seems cruel and indefensible, and yet it has been suggested that the Mute Swan would not have survived in Britain if it had been hunted and eaten like any other wild bird. Swan ownership may have saved them. Certainly there were very large numbers present throughout the middle ages. In 1553 'a small corner of the Fenland' contained 35 broods of 183 cygnets, and the many swans consumed at banquets suggests that stocks were high. Henry III's court had 125 for Christmas dinner in 1251 and, when the Archbishop of York was installed in 1466, four hundred swans were consumed.

The power of flight is not perhaps of paramount importance to the Mute Swan. It is probably the world's heaviest flying animal, and some record weights for males (22.5 kg or 49½ pounds is the highest) indicate that some individuals would have difficulty becoming airborne. Man is the adult Mute Swan's only effective enemy and, while the bird was protected by elaborate legislation, its populations did well. It is sad that, in modern times, flying wild swans are so much at risk from obstacles like power lines erected in their path.

Swans have figured in legends down the ages, their white plumage a symbol of purity. 'Swan-song' may have originated from a myth to account for migration. Swans, at least Mute Swans, do not 'sing' in the true sense, and certainly not just before they die, but the birds are particularly restless as they prepare for the journey north to their breeding grounds. Perhaps this increasing 'wing music' overhead was associated with the birds' imminent disappearance. The old Anglo-Saxon word *swan* means 'sounder' and is assumed to refer to the soughing of the wings in flight. The combination of 'Mute' and 'Swan' is therefore something of a paradox. The first element of the bird's scientific name is Greek: Cycnus was a son of Apollo by Hyria and, in the myths, both he and his mother were transformed into swans after leaping to their deaths in a lake. *Olor* is Latin for swan, and has the same root as the word in the various Celtic languages: *eala* in Irish and Scottish Gaelic, *alarch* in Welsh and *elerch* in Cornish.

The Greek myth of Leda has universal appeal. The story has it that Leda bathed in the Eurotas river in Sparta. She was spotted by Zeus, who, as soon as he touched the water, changed into a swan. Disguised thus, he seduced the girl and, nine months later, she laid two eggs out of which hatched Clytemnestra and Helen (of Troy). European legends of 'swan maidens', women who were really swans and could be captured and married if their feathery cloaks were seized and hidden, probably, like swan-songs, had their origins in the observation of migration and sought to account for the absence of these conspicuous birds during the summer.

Composers, choreographers and dancers have been inspired by the slow graceful movements of swans on still water. Anna Pavlova is best remembered for her performance of *The Dying Swan* by Saint-Saëns. *The Swan of Tuonela* by Sibelius comes from an old Finnish epic, *Kalevala*. This bird floats on the river which separates the worlds of the living and the dead and is appropriately sombre black. However, the Black Swan was not known to be other than mythical until it was discovered in January 1697 by the Dutch navigator Willem de Vlaming near what is now Perth in Western Australia. Many of the inns called the Black Swan seem to pre-date this and their signs depict Mute Swans in dark plumage.

ACKNOWLEDGEMENTS

Illustrations are acknowledged to: David Hosking, 2, 21; Eric Hosking, 1, 4, 16, 20; Eric and David Hosking, 7, 8; Roger Hosking, cover; Frank Lane Picture Agency: 10, 11 (Arthur Christianson); 13, 14 (David Grewcock); 3 (Peggy Heard); 9 (Merlyn Severn); 5 (Ronald Thompson); 12 (Roger Wilmshurst); David Platt, 6, 17, 18, 19.

Places to visit

Those who would like to know more about swans are recommended to join the Wildfowl Trust (headquarters: Slimbridge, Gloucester GL2 7BT). The Trust specialises in conserving wildfowl and their wetland habitats and has seven centres open to the public:

Arundel: The Wildfowl Trust, Mill Road, Arundel, West Sussex BN18 9PB. Telephone: Arundel (0903) 883355.
Caerlaverock: The Wildfowl Trust, Eastpark Farm, Caerlaverock, Dumfriesshire, Scotland DG1 4RS. Telephone: Glencaple (038 777) 200.
Martin Mere: The Wildfowl Trust, Martin Mere, Burscough, Ormskirk, Lancashire L40 0TA. Telephone: Burscough (0704) 895181.
Peakirk: The Wildfowl Trust, Peakirk, Peterborough, Cambridgeshire PE6 7NP. Telephone: Peterborough (0733) 252271.
Slimbridge: The Wildfowl Trust, Slimbridge, Gloucester GL2 7BT. Telephone: Cambridge, Gloucestershire (045 389) 333.
Washington: The Wildfowl Trust, District 15, Washington, Tyne and Wear NE38 8LE. Telephone: Washington (091) 4165454.
Welney: The Wildfowl Trust, Pintail House, Hundred Foot Bank, Welney, Wisbech, Cambridgeshire PE14 9TN. Telephone: Ely (0353) 860711.

The Abbotsbury swans referred to in the text may be seen at:
Abbotsbury Swannery, Abbotsbury, Dorset. Telephone: Abbotsbury (030 587) 228.

Further reading

Bacon, P. E. 'A Possible Advantage of the "Polish" Morph of the Mute Swan', *Wildfowl* 31, 51-2. 1980.
Birkhead, Mike, and Perrins, Christopher. *The Mute Swan.* Croom Helm, 1986.
Campbell, B. 'The Mute Swan Census in England and Wales 1955-56', *Bird Study* 7, 208-23. 1960.
MacSwiney, Marquis. *Six Came Flying.* Michael Joseph, 1971.
Matthews, G. V. T., and Smart, M. *Proceedings of the Second International Swan Symposium* (Sapporo, Japan). IWRB, Slimbridge, Gloucester, 1980.
Minton, C. D. T. 'Mute Swan Flocks', *Wildfowl* 22, 71-88. 1971.
Ogilvie, M. A. 'The Mute Swan in Britain 1983', *Bird Study* 33, 121-32. 1986.
Perrins, C. M., and Ogilvie, M. A. 'A Study of the Abbotsbury Mute Swans,' *Wildfowl* 32, 35-47. 1981.
Perrins, C. M., and Reynolds, C. M. 'A Preliminary Study of the Mute Swan *Cygnus olor*', *Wildfowl* 18, 74-84. 1967.
Rawcliffe, C. P. 'The Scottish Mute Swan Census 1955-56', *Bird Study* 5, 45-55. 1958.
Reynolds, C. M. 'Mute Swan Weights in Relation to Breeding Performance', *Wildfowl* 23, 111-18. 1972.
Scott, D. K. 'Winter Territoriality of Mute Swans *Cygnus olor*', *Ibis* 126, 168-76. 1984.
Scott, Peter, and the Wildfowl Trust. *The Swans.* Michael Joseph, 1971.
Ticehurst, N. F. *The Mute Swan in England.* Cleaver-Hume Press, 1957.